Ocean Extremes:
Life in the Darkest Depths and Under the Ice

by
Jonathan Kronstadt

with **Sharon Katz Cooper**
Consultant

SCHOLASTIC INC.

New York Toronto London Auckland Sydney Mexico City New Delhi Hong Kong Buenos Aires

Jonathan Kronstadt
WRITER

Jonathan writes about science, nature, and sports for children and adults. He lives in Silver Spring, Maryland, with his wife, Peggy, and children, Alison and Max.

Sharon Katz Cooper
CONSULTANT

Sharon is the education specialist for the National Museum of Natural History's Ocean Hall, set to open in 2008. She lives in Virginia with her husband, Jason, and son, Reuven.

ISBN: 0-439-71190-8

Copyright © 2005 by Scholastic Inc.

Illustrators: Shawn Gould, Yancey C. Labat, Ed Shems, Zeke Smith

Photos:

Front cover: Edie Widder. Back cover: Hugh Rose/Visuals Unlimited. Title page: Michael Van Woert/NOAA NESDIS/ORA.

Page 2: Photodisc Green (RF)/Getty Images. Page 6: (box) Edie Widder. Page 7: www.classicnatureprints.com. Page 9: (top) NOAA/NGDC; (bottom) NASA/R. Stöckli/Robert Simmon/GSFC/MODIS. Page 10: Edie Widder. Page 11: (middle) Peter Batson/imagequestmarine.com; (bottom) OAR/National Undersea Research Program (NURP). Page 12: (top and middle) Norbert Wu/Minden Pictures; (bottom) Monterey Bay Aquarium/Ann Caudle. Page 14: Kim Fulton-Bennett/MBARI. Page 15: OAR/NURP/NOAA. Page 17: (top) OAR/NURP/NOAA; (bottom) OAR/NURP/Penn State Univ. Page 18: NOAA Office of Ocean Exploration and NOAA Vents Program. Pages 19, 20, and 48: (tube worms) OAR/NURP/College of William & Mary. Pages 20 and 48: (bacteria) Carl Wirsen/WHOI; (crab and shrimp) Peter Batson/imagequestmarine.com. Pages 21 and 48: (clam) Karen L. Von Damm/National Science Foundation; (octopus) Peter Batson/imagequestmarine.com. Page 22: (top) Captain Albert E. Theberge, NOAA Corps (ret.). Pages 22 and 48: (coral) Rhian Waller/WHOI. Pages 23 and 48: (brittle star) OAR/NURP/University of South Carolina; (bottom) NOAA Office of Ocean Exploration, NOAA Vents Program, and NOAA National Marine Fisheries Service. Page 24: (top) MBARI; (middle and bottom) Norbert Wu. Page 25: Craig Smith. Page 26: (Pawson) Smithsonian Institution; (Scotoplanes) David Wrobel/Visuals Unlimited. Page 27: (top) Ken Lucas/Visuals Unlimited; (bottom) Edie Widder. Pages 28 and 29: Edie Widder. Page 34: Norbert Wu. Page 39: (top) Michael S. Nolan/ SeaPics.com; (middle) Ingrid Visser/SeaPics.com; (bottom) Charles George/Visuals Unlimited. Pages 40 and 42: (polar bears) Fritz Polking/Visuals Unlimited. Page 42: (bottom) Saul Gonor/SeaPics.com. Page 43: (top) Steve Maxson; (middle) Richard Herrmann/Visuals Unlimited; (bottom) Mark Conlin/SeaPics.com. Page 44: (top) Hal Brindley/V & W/SeaPics.com; (bottom) Rick Price/Corbis. Page 45: (top) W. Perry Conway/Corbis; (middle) Fritz Poelking/V & W/SeaPics.com. Page 46: Hal Brindley/V & W/SeaPics.com. Page 47: (top) Katrin Iken/University of Alaska Fairbanks; (bottom) Rolf Gradinger/University of Alaska Fairbanks; (fish) NOAA.

12 11 10 9 8 7 6 5 4 3 2 1   5 6 7 8 9/0

Printed in the U.S.A.

First Scholastic printing, June 2005

The publisher has made every effort to ensure that the activities in this book are safe when done as instructed. Adults should provide guidance and supervision whenever the activity requires.

Table of Contents

page 30

page 32

page 35

Deepest, Darkest,

You, ocean explorer, are about to journey to the extremes of the ocean—
to the ocean's deepest and coldest places—where the conditions are so dark,
icy, and just plain miserable, it seems like life could never survive. But it does!
And you're about to meet some of the amazing creatures that manage to thrive
in these strange worlds. As you explore, you'll find the answers to questions like:

- How deep *is* the ocean?

It sure is deep here!

- What kinds of creatures live in
  the deepest parts of the ocean?

I can stand the pressure!

- How do animals survive way down deep,
  where the water pressure is *really* high?

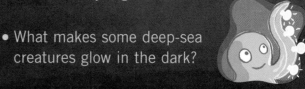

- What makes some deep-sea
  creatures glow in the dark?

It's tough to find a good meal!

- Why is it so hard to survive
  at the extremes?

what's that?

- What's a black
  smoker?

- How can animals live without
  light from the Sun?

Hey! Who put a ceiling here?

- How can animals survive
  living under a sheet of ice?

- How do sea creatures keep from freezing
  in super-cold water?

and Coldest
Life at the Extremes!

Extreme Places, Amazing Animals

You won't believe where these pages will take you—or what you'll see when you get there. At the ocean's deepest depths and under the ice, you'll discover enough fascinating creatures to fill, well, an ocean! Along the way, you'll find out how these amazing animals have adapted to such extreme conditions.

In the deepest seas and along the ocean floor, you'll discover wonders like:

- fish that can swallow animals bigger than themselves.

- tiny organisms that turn poisonous chemicals into food.

- thousands of deep-sea creatures that feed off the remains of a whale.

After you've gone as deep as you can go, you'll venture under the ice to discover what life is like for animals that live in chilly Arctic and Antarctic waters. There, you'll be amazed by:

- fish with their own natural form of anti-freeze.

- the world's biggest meat-eater.

- places where there's so much food, it changes the color of the ocean.

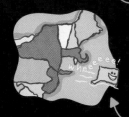

- places where there's so little food, some creatures will eat members of their own species!

- icebergs the size of Connecticut!

That's just a taste of the wonders you'll see on your journey to the extremes. So let's get going!

What's in Your Undersea Kit?

Your Undersea Kit positively glows with possibilities! Here's what you've got:

Three Glow Sticks

Many creatures who live in the ocean's deepest, darkest places have found ways to make their own light. With these glow sticks, you can see what it's like to communicate and find food with light, just like a deep-sea fish. Your glow sticks will stay lit for about eight hours, so don't bend them until you're ready to use them. Flip to page 30 to get started!

Glow-in-the-Dark Fish Kit

You can create your own glowing fish with this collection of stickers and reusable sheets of black paper. Check out page 32 for some design ideas!

Iceberg Mold

Have you ever heard the expression "that's only the tip of the iceberg"? Find out what that means by making your own iceberg and watching it float! Just head to page 35 to go polar!

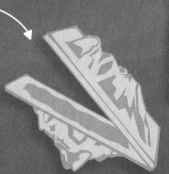

The Undersea University Website

For more fun with ocean extremes, swim over to the Undersea website at **www.scholastic.com/undersea**. Dive in with the password on the right to *deepen* your sea smarts!

WEB-SURFING PASSWORD

DEEPCOLD

PART I: The Darkest Depths

You'll start your journey to the extremes by plunging way, way down to the darkest depths, where you'll come face to face with all sorts of deep-sea creatures. Get ready for the low-down on what's down below!

What Do We Know About the Darkest Depths?

Until about 150 years ago, people knew almost nothing about the deep sea. Many people believed the ocean was bottomless and the deep sea was lifeless. Others thought huge sea serpents lurked there. But in the 1870s scientists began dipping nets down deep to collect samples, discovering all sorts of amazing creatures (but no man-eating sea monsters). Then, in the early 1900s, sonar was invented, which sent sound waves bouncing off the ocean bottom and gave scientists some ideas of how the ocean floor was shaped.

The most famous expedition was the HMS *Challenger*, which spent four years during the 1870s bringing up nets from the depths of the ocean. The scientists found 4,717 new species—everything from octopuses to strange-looking fish—and filled fifty books with drawings and descriptions of everything they found! The *Challenger* got the world really excited about the ocean floor, and scientists haven't stopped exploring since.

What's It Like Down There?

If you drain a swimming pool, you end up with a big, flat pit. But what would you find if you drained the ocean? Actually, the ground beneath all that water is a lot like the ground on the rest of the planet—it's got plains, valleys, mountains, and more. Check it out for yourself in the Sea Quest on the next page!

Artists carefully sketched the amazing creatures the *Challenger* brought up from the depths. Here you can see a strange-looking octopus.

See the Seafloor!

It wasn't until about thirty years ago that the first map of the world's ocean floor was created. It showed an amazing array of mountains and valleys, plains and volcanoes. In this Sea Quest, you'll find features like these for yourself in the map on the right. But first, you'll need to identify their locations using *longitude* and *latitude*, the same measurements scientists use to pinpoint a location anywhere on Earth!

Before You Start

How do longitude and latitude work? Here's a primer.

- **Longitude** measures where something is on the Earth in terms of east and west. Think of the Earth as a peeled orange; the longitude lines are the separations between the orange sections. Zero degrees longitude is at the *prime meridian*, which runs from the North Pole to the South Pole through England, Europe, and West Africa. Everything to the east of the prime meridian is measured in degrees *east longitude*, and everything to its west is measured in degrees *west longitude*.

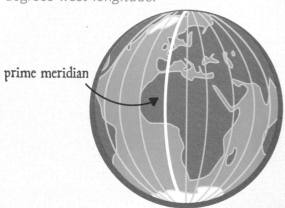

prime meridian

- **Latitude** measures how far north or south a spot on the Earth is. Zero degrees latitude is at the *equator*, which goes right around the middle of the Earth.

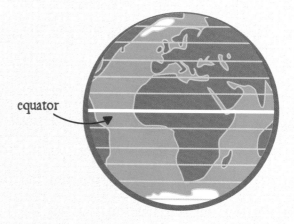

equator

- Any spot on the Earth has a measurement in degrees longitude and latitude, and these numbers combined are called *coordinates*. You'll be using coordinates to locate the ocean floor features you find.

- Oh, and one more hint about the map on the right: The deeper the ocean, the darker the blue!

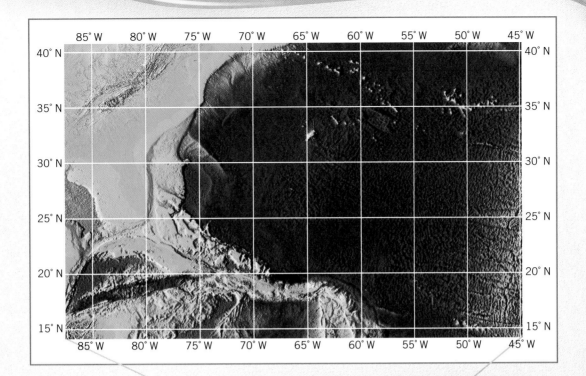

What You Do

For each question below, figure out which coordinates point to the correct feature on the map above. You can check your answers on page 48!

I. A **ridge** is like a mountain range on the ocean floor. Which of these coordinates is a spot on the Mid-Atlantic Ridge? Hint: Look at the full world map for help!

A. 30° N and 60° W

B. 20° N and 46° W

C. 40° N and 71° W

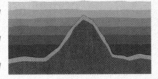

2. Trenches are big valleys on the ocean floor. They're long, narrow, and deep. Which of these spots is in the Puerto Rico Trench?

A. 33° N and 75° W

B. 18° N and 60° W

C. 21° N and 70° W

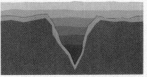

3. Seamounts are underwater mountains. Which of these coordinates points to the New England Seamounts?

A. 23° N and 68° W

B. 38° N and 60° W

C. 30° N and 68° W

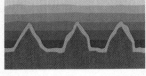

4. The **continental shelf** is a high part of the ocean floor along the edge of a contintent. Which spot is on the continental shelf?

A. 20° N and 85° W

B. 25° N and 75° W

C. 37° N and 75° W

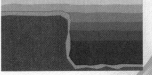

Going Down, Down, Down

Now that you've seen what the ocean floor looks like, it's time to dive down to the deepest, darkest reaches and find out what it's like to *live* down there! The creatures who live in the deep sea are experts at *adaptation*, which in this case means they've managed to make the best of a tough situation.

Living Without Light

Sunlight rarely reaches more than 650 feet (198 m) down—but the ocean goes all the way down to 39,000 feet (11,700 m) in some places! This means that the depths of the ocean are *very* cold and dark. The water of the deep sea stays just a few degrees above freezing, around 39 degrees F (4 degrees C), so deep-sea creatures have to find ways to stay warm. And unlike the creatures that live near the sunlit surface of the ocean, deep-sea animals can't see their food swimming through clear, blue water around them. In the darkest depths, sea creatures have to use other senses to detect their food—or make their own light!

Pressing Needs

Living under all that water *also* means that deep-sea creatures have lots and lots of water pressing down on them. At the deepest spot in the ocean, the pressure is 8 tons per square inch! But the creatures who live down there have found ways to manage.

Deep-sea creatures also have to find ways to stay fed in spite of scarce food. It's a challenge at the bottom of the ocean, because plants can't grow where there's no light, and there aren't many animals to serve as prey. This means the animals that live down there have to stay on the lookout for whatever there is to eat—and then make it last. You'll find out how on page 12!

deep-sea squid

deep-sea fish

One reason the creatures of the deep look so weird is because they have to deal with some of the most unusual conditions on the planet!

Who Turned Off the Lights —and the Heat?

If you tried to live at the bottom of the ocean, you'd get really cold really fast. And *forget* looking around for a warm meal—even if there *were* underwater cafeterias, you'd have a tough time finding one in the pitch-black water! So how do deep-sea creatures survive? Read on!

Surviving the Chill Challenge

Sperm whales are the champions of cold-water diving. These massive mammals have been known to dive for up to two hours without stopping, covering almost two miles—straight down! They stay warm with a layer of blubber that can be a foot thick.

sperm whale

Left in the Dark

If you've ever fumbled around a dark kitchen in the middle of the night looking for that cookie you're *positive* you left on the counter, you know what deep-sea creatures have to go through every time they get hungry! Some of them use senses other than sight to get lunch. **Sea cucumbers** have tentacles that work like tiny hands to scoop mud into their mouths as they crawl along the seafloor. **Siphonophores**, relatives of jellies, just spread out and sting anything that comes in contact with their tentacles.

sea cucumber

By far the most popular method of finding food in the dark is to make your own light. It's called *bioluminescence*, and you'll learn all about it on page 27!

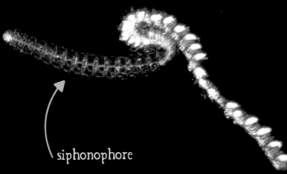

siphonophore

Lots of Pressure, Little Food

It's hard enough living in the cold and the dark—but these aren't the *only* problems deep-sea creatures have to deal with! Read on to find out how they've adapted to the high pressure and the lack of food way down deep.

Handling the Pressure

You know the pressure you feel on your ears when you swim to the bottom of a swimming pool? Multiply that by a few hundred and you'll start to get an idea of the kind of pressure deep-sea creatures live with all the time.

Most deep-dwelling animals, like **comb jellies**, can cope with the pressure because their bodies are filled with water, instead of with air like other creatures. Water can stand up to pressure much better than air. These animals also have no bones or skeletons that could be crushed.

Other creatures, like the **giant sea isopod**, have such strong shells that the pressure doesn't bother them. These guys are related to the little pill bugs you sometimes find under rocks—except that these creatures are often a foot long!

comb jelly

giant sea isopod

orange roughy

Isn't It Lunchtime Yet?

Since they never know when their next meal is coming, animals in the deep sea digest their food very, very slowly. Because of this, everything that goes on in their bodies happens slower than in other creatures, including aging—so deep-sea creatures often live extra-long lives. The **orange roughy**, a deep-sea fish that many people eat, can live for 150 years. This means people could be eating something older than their grandparents!

Piling Up the Pressure

What You Need

- Empty 2-liter plastic soda bottle
- Scissors
- Tape
- Water
- Sink

Your Crew

- An adult

You just found out how some animals cope with the intense pressure—*water* pressure, that is—that comes with living in the deep sea. Try this Sea Quest and you'll see for yourself how the pressure rises as you go deeper!

What You Do

1. Have an adult cut three small holes on one side of an empty 2-liter plastic soda bottle: one near the top, one in the middle, and one at the bottom.

2. Cover all three holes with a single strip of tape.

3. Fill the bottle with water to the top and place it in a sink.

4. Now, quickly pull off the strip of tape and watch how the streams of water flow out of each hole. What differences do you see? How do the streams change as more and more water flows out of the bottle?

Sea the Point?

You should have noticed that the water coming from the bottom hole streamed out faster and went out farther than the streams higher up. Why? Since there was more water above the bottom hole, there was more pressure to push that water out. As the water flowed out, the streams should have all slowed down, because the pressure was getting lower as water left the bottle.

This means that the more water there is above you, the more water pressure is on you. It's a lot like being at the bottom of a pile of kids: The more weight that's on top of you, the more pressure you feel (and the louder you yell at everyone to get off!). But unlike you, ocean explorer, deep-sea creatures have adaptations to live comfortably under the pressures of the depths.

HEY! I'm getting SQUISHED!

The pressure feels okay to me!

Contents Under Pressure

Because deep-sea fish are so well adapted to high pressure, they can't survive if they're captured and brought up to the surface, where the pressure is so much lower. But it's important for scientists to be able to study these fish while they're alive.

To solve this problem, a new high-pressure "fish trap" is being developed by researchers at the Monterey Bay Aquarium Research Institute. The trap will capture fish at the bottom of the ocean, then keep the water and fish inside it under high pressure while the trap rises to the surface. This should keep the fish inside alive.

The trap could also allow the pressure around the fish to change very, very slowly. If a fish adapted to these slow pressure changes and stayed alive, it could be displayed at aquariums. Who knows, ocean explorer—some day you might see some of the weirdest, wildest deep-sea creatures swimming right in front of you—while you're still on land!

floats help trap rise after collecting fish

fish are trapped in here

The walls of this high-pressure fish trap are up to 3 inches (8 cm) thick to withstand high pressure.

Your Seafloor Tour

Deep-sea creatures have lots in common—they can all stand up to high pressure and darkness—but the places where they live can be very different. As you saw on pages 8–9, the ocean floor is covered in mountains, plains, trenches, and more. You're about to take a tour of some of the most interesting spots (starting here and ending on page 25). Along the way, you'll meet the weird and wild creatures that live in each place. First stop: volcanic vents in the ocean floor!

Life without Light

Until 1977, scientists believed that all forms of life, from the tiniest microbe to the biggest whale, depended on the Sun for energy like heat and light. Without the Sun, plants couldn't grow, and without plants, animals couldn't eat. But then the first *hydrothermal vent* was discovered, and all that changed.

What are hydrothermal vents? Well, *hydro* means "water," and *thermal* means "heat." So when heated water comes rushing up through an opening in the ocean floor, you've got a hydrothermal vent!

They happen like this: First, cold water seeps down through cracks in the ocean floor. Then, this water is super-heated by incredibly hot liquid rock. Finally, the water spurts back up into the ocean, mixed with minerals from the liquid rock below. The water can be as hot as 680 degrees F (360 degrees C)! The minerals in the water help support the animals nearby. The creatures around a vent make up one of the only food webs on Earth that survives and grows without depending on plants—and just wait till you see some of these creatures on pages 18–21!

water rushing up from a hydrothermal vent

Where There's Smoke, There's Water?

Hydrothermal vents are one of nature's most recently discovered wonders, but now you can make one in your own kitchen. Try this Sea Quest and discover exactly how a bubbling deep-sea vent works!

What You Need

- Baby food jar, with the label removed
- Piece of string, 18 inches (46 cm) long
- Red and green food coloring
- Warm water
- Large, clear pitcher or vase
- Cold water

What You Do

1. Start by making a handle around a baby food jar. First, tie one end of a string in a loop around the mouth of the jar. Then tie the other end of the string around the mouth with its knot on the opposite side of the first one, creating a handle.

2. Put a couple drops of red and green food coloring in the baby food jar (to make black), then fill it with warm water.

3. Fill a large pitcher with cold water up to about 3 inches (8 cm) from the top.

4. Using the string handle, lower the jar into the cold water and watch what happens!

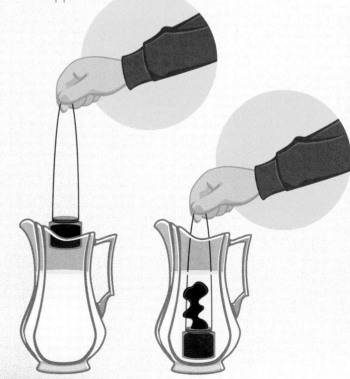

Sea the Point?

The dark warm water rose up quickly once it hit the cold water, right? This is exactly what happens in a hydrothermal vent. Heat rises, so when water becomes super-heated by hot melted rock under the ocean floor, it spurts up like a geyser. The water takes on the color of the minerals, metals, and other stuff that it carries on its way up.

The hottest hydrothermal vents spew out water mixed with tiny particles of metal and other dark minerals from the hot liquid rock below. This mixture looks like black smoke, and these vents are called *black smokers*. There are also *white smokers*, which spew out a mix of white minerals, such as calcium and silicon (a mineral found in sand).

When the dissolved particles of either color of water settle out, chimneys are formed around where the water spurts out. Some of these chimneys can grow as fast as 12 inches (30 cm) a day and can reach as high as 150 feet (46 m)—that's as high as a 15-story building!

white smoker

Cold, Deep Seeps

Hot water isn't the only thing that comes up through the ocean floor—cold water seeps up, too! *Cold seeps* are areas where cool, energy-rich gases and fluids ooze their way through the ocean floor, attracting animals that look a lot like the ones that hang out near hydrothermal vents. Scientists are still trying to figure out why many of the same kinds of species turn up at both the hot and cold ocean floor faucets.

This colony of tube worms is clustered around a cold seep. You'll see the same kind of creatures at a hydrothermal vent on the next page!

Living the Vent Life

Now that you know how hydrothermal vents work, it's time to meet the creatures that live around them. And there are lots! Just like people gather around fires to keep warm when they're out camping, deep-sea creatures on the ocean floor gather around hydrothermal vents. But instead of heat, these sea creatures are there for *food*. There's 500 times more food around hydrothermal vents than there is around other parts of the ocean floor. Why? Mostly because of some amazing bacteria.

Single Cell Superstars

At first, scientists couldn't figure out how so many animals could survive around a hydrothermal vent when there seemed to be so little food there. Then they discovered that the vents were home to bacteria—living things made of just one cell (that's as small and simple as life gets). These bacteria, which live close to the source of the vent, can survive in temperatures as high as 250 degrees F (121 degrees C). No other known organism can survive in temperatures that high!

Vent bacteria use the poisonous chemicals that come out of the vents as a source of energy to create the sugars they need to live. Animals eat the bacteria, and these creatures get eaten by bigger creatures, creating a food web that exists without any energy from the Sun.

Vents are crowded with bacteria, shrimp, clams, crabs, and more. In fact, many scientists think that the areas around vents have more life per cubic foot than anywhere else on the planet!

shrimp

mussels

Mussels, crabs, and shrimp
around a hydrothermal vent

crabs

A Live-In Food Source

One of the biggest—and strangest—creatures that lives around hydrothermal vents is the **giant tube worm**. Unlike the worms in your backyard, this worm can grow up to 4 feet (1.2 m) long. It has no mouth and no stomach. How does it eat? Vent bacteria grow inside its body, making food from the vent's chemicals and releasing this food right into the worm's body!

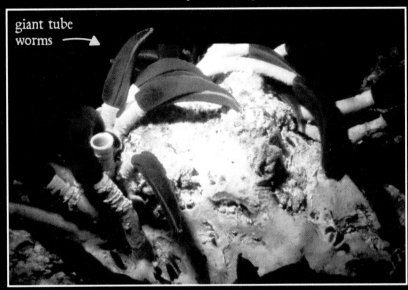

giant tube worms

Going, Going...

Vents only last for a few decades before water stops rushing up through them and they go "extinct." When this happens, the animals around them have to find new homes. Scientists still don't know how these creatures find new vents, but they *do* know that vent creatures reproduce quickly and have lots of babies. That way, at least a few of them will be able to find new homes and survive if the vent goes extinct.

Vents Around the Universe

Researchers are especially interested in vents because they may hold the key to finding other life forms in other places that aren't lit or warmed by the Sun—like distant planets and moons!

Some astrobiologists (scientists who study the possibility of life in outer space) believe that if there is life on other planets, it's probably a lot like vent bacteria—able to stand extreme temperatures and turn poisonous chemicals into energy and food. Some scientists also believe that life began on Earth in an extreme environment, and that the study of vent bacteria may hold the key to unlocking the mystery of our planet's first life forms.

Figure Out the Food Web

What You Need
- Your food-web wisdom

You met your first hydrothermal vent creatures on the last two pages. But what *other* animals live around a vent—and which animals eat which? Even scientists don't know for sure, but they've got some pretty good guesses. Try this Sea Quest to see how your guesses compare!

What You Do

Below, you'll find six different animals who live around hydrothermal vents. Read about each one, then write its name in the right spot in the Vent Food Web on the right. One has already been done for you. You can check your answers on page 48!

I. Vent bacteria. These single-celled sea creatures turn toxic chemicals into food.

2. Vent crab. There are so many crabs around hydrothermal vents that the pilots of the famous submersible *Alvin* know that when they see vent crabs, a vent is nearby. These crabs have a great sense of smell, which helps them find the creatures they like to eat. But they're not above eating some of the tiniest forms of life around the vents, either.

3. Tube worm. No mouth, no eyes, and no stomach means there's no way this animal can get food on its own. But that doesn't mean it doesn't eat and grow—its meals are produced inside its body.

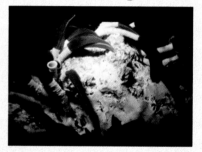

4. Vent shrimp. These shrimp swarm near vent chimneys, and they even have light-sensitive patches on their backs that guide them toward the very faint glow vents give off. There's no shortage of food for shrimp around vents, but these little creatures are likely to *be* food if they don't keep an eye out for snapping claws!

5. Vent clam. Like tube worms, these creatures have live-in food. They grow as big as your shoe in between mounds of volcanic rock near vents, and they make a good meal for two of the other creatures here!

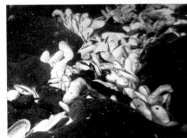

6. Octopus. The biggest and most dangerous predator at the vent, this octopus's arms probably stay busy snatching up the shelled creatures it likes to eat.

Vent Food Web

Octopus

eats *eats* *eats* *eats* *eats* *eats* *eats*

Sea Mountaineering

What's big, tall, rocky, and cone-shaped? If you said a mountain, you're right—but what if that mountain rises straight up from the ocean floor and doesn't reach the ocean's surface? Then you've got a *seamount*!

Seamounts are underwater mountains that usually start out as active volcanoes, though most stopped erupting long ago. Because they stick up high above the ocean floor, seamounts create currents in the water that bring food (like plankton) up to the mount. This extra food helps seamounts support a huge variety of creatures!

Living on the Edge

Seamounts' rocky slopes are perfect for deep-sea corals and other animals that like to attach themselves to hard surfaces. The corals in turn provide a habitat for all kinds of creatures, from sponges and sea stars to fish.

In this illustration of the ocean floor, you can see Davidson Seamount, which was the first underwater mountain scientists officially called a "seamount."

Seamounts are home to animals that don't live anywhere else in the ocean. One seamount might even have creatures that don't exist on any *other* seamount! This means that the discovery of a new seamount could mean the discovery of new creatures, too.

What's New in New England?

The New England Seamounts, which you found in the Sea Quest on pages 8–9, are a chain of about twenty-five extinct volcanoes off the east coast of North America. Scientists have visited these seamounts and collected samples of the deep-sea corals growing there. By examining the corals' skeletons, scientists hope to learn how climate and water temperature in that area changed throughout Earth's history—and with this information, they can try to figure out what's in store for the future!

The coral shown here is one of the types of coral scientists collected from the New England Seamounts. Unlike shallow-water coral, this coral lives deep underwater, in total darkness.

The Flattest Part of the Floor

Chances are if you're at the bottom of the deep sea, you're on an *abyssal plain*. *Abyssal* comes from the word "abyss," which means an incredibly deep place. These plains make up 60 percent of the ocean bottom, and like most plains, they're pretty flat.

Unlike most plains, however, abyssal plains are covered with thick, soft ooze (that's really what scientists call it!) that can be up to several *thousand* feet deep. This ooze is made up of the remains of dead plants and animals that drift down from the ocean above, including plankton, particles that wash off land into the sea, and maybe even dust from outer space.

To live on top of a big pile of mud, it helps to be lightweight and to spread out, so you don't sink into the ooze. **Brittle stars** do exactly that, which makes the abyssal plains a great home for them.

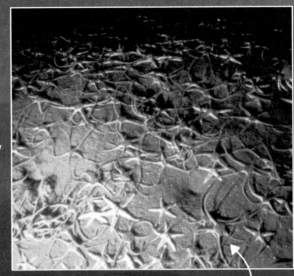

brittle stars

sea cucumbers

That's One Big Salad

A **sea cucumber's** favorite breakfast—and lunch, and dinner—is mud. And the abyssal plains have all the mud they could ask for! This might explain why sea cucumbers make up around 90 percent of the total weight of animals that live on the seafloor. There are more than 1,200 different species of sea cucumbers, the biggest of which is about six feet long. And many of them can do amazing things, like eject most of their internal organs to confuse predators, then regrow them when the threat is gone!

My, What Big Teeth You Have!

The ocean floor has plenty of food for mud-eating animals (like the sea cucumbers on the previous page)—but if you're a creature who eats *fish* for your meals, food can be hard to find. That's why the predators who hang out near the deep-sea floor are some of the creepiest, hungriest-looking creatures in the world. Here are some of the special features that help them get the food they need:

- Big eyes—eating opportunities don't swim by very often, and even when they do, it's dark, so it helps to have enormous eyes. The **vampire squid** is just 6 inches (15 cm) long, but it has eyes as big as a large dog's.

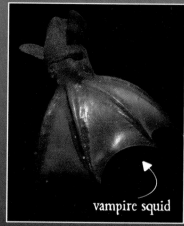
vampire squid

fangtooth

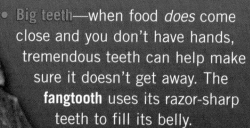

- Big teeth—when food *does* come close and you don't have hands, tremendous teeth can help make sure it doesn't get away. The **fangtooth** uses its razor-sharp teeth to fill its belly.

- A big mouth—one rule in the deep sea is: Just because it's bigger than you doesn't mean you can't eat it. Not only does this **gulper eel** have a huge mouth, it can unhinge its jaw to make sure that its food, no matter how big, fits in.

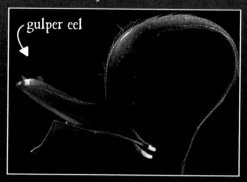
gulper eel

If you don't have the skills—or the sharp teeth—to go chasing after your own food, you may have to wait for your food to come to you. That's exactly what some deep-sea creatures do! Read on to find out how!

Whale Falls Mean Food for All

This whale, which is surrounded by worm-shaped fish called hagfish, has been on the ocean floor for just six weeks.

When a giant tree falls to the forest floor, it provides food for a wide variety of animals. The same thing happens when a whale falls to the deep-sea floor!

Oceanographer Craig Smith was the first to discover what are called "whale falls" off the Southern California coast in 1987. Once a dead whale has settled on the ocean floor, scavengers like sharks and hagfish are the first to come and feed on the whale's flesh, which can last for a few months.

After the whale's flesh is all gone, there's still more than enough nourishment for a small world of worms, mussels, and snails to live on. And as the whale decays, it produces the same kind of chemicals as those found at hydrothermal vents—and it attracts the same kind of bacteria!

In one case, 5,098 animals were found on less than one square yard of dead whale. And whale bones are so rich in oil that they can support a community of animals for decades!

After four and a half years, these whale bones are covered in layers of red and white bacteria.

Do-It-Yourself Whale Falls

It's hard for scientists to study whale falls because they have to *find* these fallen whales, first. To make things easier, they sometimes sink whales that have died stranded on beaches. That way, they know exactly where to go to visit the whale fall. But it can be hard to sink a whale that doesn't sink of natural causes! Scientists often have to attach as much as 6,600 pounds (3,000 kg) of metal weight to the whale to get it to sink.

MARINE BIOLOGIST
Dr. David L. Pawson

Dr. David L. Pawson is a marine biologist at the Smithsonian's National Museum of Natural History. His research focuses on the Echinoderms (sea stars, sea cucumbers, and their relatives). He is especially interested in the deep sea, and he has made more than 100 dives in underwater vehicles called *submersibles*, in search of the animals he studies.

David Pawson unloading a container of creatures from a submersible

Question: What's it like being 13,000 feet (3,962 m) below the surface of the ocean inside a submersible?

Answer: It's an amazing experience! When you get to the bottom, it's completely dark, and then the lights are turned on and you look out of your window to see what wonderful and exciting things the light has revealed—you might see a sea cucumber, or a fish sitting on the bottom, or a red shrimp swimming by. You might even see animals that have never been seen before!

Q: Do you have a favorite deep-sea creature?

A: My favorite deep-sea creature today (it may change tomorrow) is the sea cucumber called a *Scotoplanes* (SKO-toe-play-knees). With its little legs and its rounded body, it looks like a little pig snuffling on the seafloor!

Scotoplanes

Q: Why are there so many sea cucumbers on the deep ocean floor?

A: The mud on the ocean floor has very slowly built up over millions of years from the dead bodies of tiny animals and plants that lived near the ocean surface. To an animal that eats mud for a living—such as a sea cucumber—this muddy ocean floor is like a paradise! So, millions and billions of sea cucumbers live down there, picking up the mud with their feeding tentacles and stuffing it into their mouths.

Q: What's the strangest thing you've ever discovered on the seafloor?

A: Perhaps it was *The New York Times* newspaper, lying on the seafloor about 9,000 feet (2,743 m) below the surface, spread out very neatly, and in perfect condition, so that we could read the date on the newspaper—it was two months old!

Light Alert!

As you learned on page 11, sunlight reaches just 650 feet (198 m) below the ocean's surface on average, so everything below that is pretty much pitch black. In fact, it would be *completely* pitch black if it weren't for a lot of sea creatures that make their *own* light!

When deep-sea animals produce their own light, it's called *bioluminescence* (*bio* means "life," and *luminescence* means "light"). For humans who visit the deep, bioluminescence creates an amazing light show. But for the deep-sea creatures who light up, it's a matter of survival, as you'll see on the next page!

How Does Bioluminescence Work?

Most of the light you see, including the light from fire, light bulbs, and sunlight, is a form of energy that comes from heat. But the light that animals create through bioluminescence is energy that comes from a chemical reaction, with no heat involved. That's why fireflies are cool enough to touch. Deep-sea fish create the same kind of "cold light," and so do the glow sticks that came in your Undersea Kit.

Some creatures glow because they have glowing bacteria living inside certain parts of their bodies. **Flashlight fish** have large light-up spots under each eye, created by bacteria that live inside. These fish have muscle flaps that they use like window shades to cover and uncover their lights. When the spot is covered, the light produces a pale green glow that attracts prey. When the fish is threatened by a predator, it uncovers its light to blind the predator long enough to make a getaway.

flashlight fish

Most bioluminescent fish create the chemicals they need to glow from the food they eat. These chemicals are combined to create light inside organs called *photophores*. In the Sea Quest on page 30, you'll see for yourself how chemicals can create light!

viperfish

The photophores along the viperfish's belly help it disguise itself in the open ocean, because it blends into the lighter water above it.

Life with Light

You've probably seen bioluminescence in fireflies, but they're one of the few land-dwelling creatures that can light up. On the other hand, scientists estimate that nine out of ten deep-sea animals are bioluminescent. Why is glowing so popular down deep? Well, you can do lots of things by lighting up, like...

1. Catch Food

Anglerfish catch their food with the help of a long, thin fin with a glowing tip. This fin works just like a fishing lure. Small sea creatures are attracted to the anglerfish's light—and before they know what's going on, they're lunch!

anglerfish

deep-sea jelly
in darkness

deep-sea jelly
lit by camera

2. Avoid Becoming Food

When a bioluminescent **deep-sea jelly** is attacked, it lights up in what scientists call a "burglar alarm." Why? It's hoping that a bigger fish will see its glow, then come over and eat whatever's trying to eat *it*!

Some **deep-sea shrimp** also use bioluminescence to stay safe from predators. When attacked, they spew glowing vomit to blind the predator, then hurry out of the way.

deep-sea shrimp

viperfish attacking

3. Stay Out of Sight

If you're swimming in the ocean and you look up at a fish from beneath, it might stand out as a dark outline against the bright sunlit water above it. That's why many fish have lights on their bellies to blend in! Lights like these are called *counterillumination*. The **hatchetfish** can even dim its lights to stay hidden when the Sun goes behind a cloud.

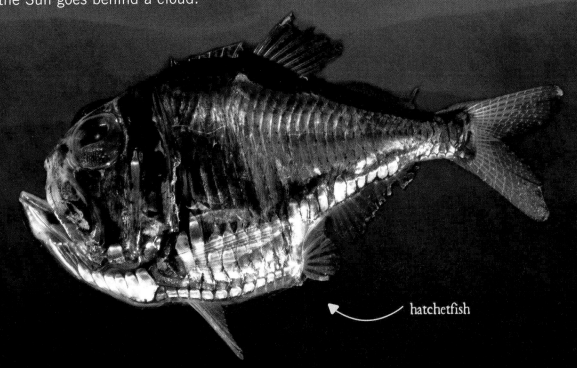

hatchetfish

I Can See You, But You Can't See Me

Blue light travels a long way underwater (that's why deep water looks dark blue), but red light doesn't make it very far. Because red colors don't make it far in the deep sea, most deep-dwelling creatures have eyes that can't see red light at all. That means that red shrimp, red fish, and red light all register to these creatures as nothing but black.

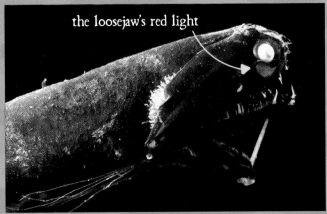

the loosejaw's red light

Loosejaw fish are some of the only deep-sea fish that can see red light—and create it! Loosejaw fish shine red light into the ocean around them to search for prey. But their prey won't see them, because the red light is completely invisible to them!

Light the Way!

Now that you've read all about how and why deep-sea animals light up, it's time to find out what it's really like to be bioluminescent. Try this Sea Quest, and you'll see how handy light can be when it comes to finding food and communicating with other fish!

Sea Quest

What You Need

- Aluminum foil
- Scissors
- Glow sticks UNDERSEA UNIVERSITY

Your crew

- 2 friends

What You Do

Part 1: Find Some Food

A little light can go a long way when it comes to finding food. See for yourself!

1. First, gently crinkle up some aluminum foil into a loose ball. Then uncrinkle it and lay it flat.

2. Cut out five small fish from your wrinkled foil.

3. Have a friend go into another room and place your fish around the room (but not under things—leave them out in the open). You should stay away until your friend is done!

4. Have your friend turn off the lights, making the room as dark as possible. Now, enter the dark room. Look around and see how long it takes you to find the fish—*if* you can find them in the dark!

5. After you've found them (or after you give up), leave the room and have your friend place the fish in different places.

6. This time, bring your blue glow stick into the room along with you! (It's the one that looks clear—it will turn blue when it lights up.) To activate your stick, bend it along its entire length, until it's glowing all over.

7. Enter the room again with your glow stick. See how long it takes you to find the fish now!

Part 2: Find Some Friends

Lights aren't just a great way to find food—they're also a good way to communicate! Want to try it out? Read on.

1. Activate your remaining two glow sticks by cracking them, then give them to two friends.

2. Each of you should decide to flash one of the codes below, but don't tell the others what you've decided!

1) short-short-LONG, short-short-LONG

2) LONG-LONG-short, LONG-LONG-short

3. Now, turn off all the lights or go into a dark room. Fold your glow stick into a loop and hold the ends in your fist, with the curved part sticking out. Using your free hand to cover the glow stick, uncover and re-cover the light quickly to flash your pattern at your friends. Everyone should watch each other. Can you figure out who's flashing the same pattern you are?

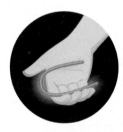

covered

uncovered

Sea the Point?

Congratulations—you just demonstrated a couple of ways that animals use bioluminescence in the ocean! In Part 1, you found "food" using light. Lots of animals use the light they produce to find food in the darkness of the deep. Most of the time they use blue light like you did. As you read on page 29, blue light travels the farthest through water. But bioluminescence can take on any color. Your glow sticks came in three different colors so that you can imitate whatever kind of fish you want!

In Part 2, you matched patterns of flashing light. It's so dark in the depths of the ocean that it's hard to tell who belongs to your species and who doesn't. That's why many animals use these same kinds of flashing patterns to identify potential mates.

So, what exactly makes your glow sticks glow? Believe it or not, it's the same thing that makes fish glow! In both cases, light is created by a chemical reaction that happens when two different chemicals combine. In your glow sticks, these two chemicals were stored in two different compartments inside your sticks. When you cracked them, the chemicals mixed together and light was produced!

The chemical reaction will continue inside your glow stick for hours, until the energy is all used up. Fish combine chemicals themselves inside their *photophores*, creating light. Unlike your glow stick, fish continuously create the chemicals they need, so they can glow whenever they want.

Want more glow-stick fun? Wrap one of your glow sticks around you wrist, connecting the two ends with one of the small plastic connectors that came in your Undersea Kit. You've now got a glowing bracelet! Or is that a bioluminescent lure at the end of your arm?

glow-stick connector

Glow with the Flow

Some deep-sea fish use light to lure in their prey, but others use light to keep from *being* prey! These fish have glowing spots along their bodies

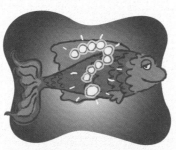

that confuse predators—in the dark, predators just see a bunch of little lights instead of one big fish. With your Glow-in-the-Dark Fish Kit, you'll create your own glowing fish and other creatures, then see how they look when you turn out the lights!

What You Need
- Paper and pencil
- Scissors
- Glow-in-the-Dark Fish Kit
- Desk lamp

Your Crew
- A friend

What You Do

Part 1: Fish in Disguise

Ready to create your own glowing fish? With your Glow-in-the-Dark Fish Kit and the fish outlines below, you've got everything you need to get started!

1. Trace the fish shape below onto a piece of paper.

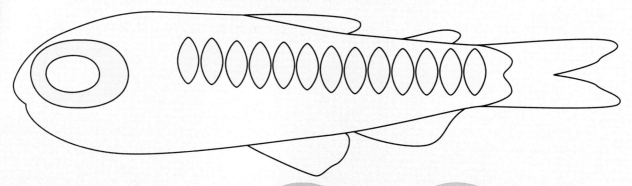

2. Cut the fish out and place the glow-in-the-dark stickers from your Undersea Kit on the fish as shown.

3. Place the fish under a desk lamp for a few minutes to charge up the glow-in-the-dark stickers.

4. Now turn off all the lights and make sure the room is as dark as possible. What does your fish look like, now that all you can see is the places where it glows?

5. Bring a friend into the dark room and have your friend draw what the fish might look like, based on the glowing parts. Then turn the lights back on and see how the drawing compares to the real fish!

6. Repeat steps 1–5 for the fish outline below. For more outlines, you can head over to the Undersea U website at **www.scholastic.com/undersea**.

Part 2: Create Your Own!

Now that you've seen how some real fish look when there's no light, create some of your own disguised fish!

I. Using the black paper from your Undersea Kit, cut out your own ideas for fish, squid, or other undersea creatures.

2. Now place the stickers anywhere you want—it's up to you! Your stickers can be moved around on the black paper as many times as needed. Then turn off the lights and see how different your creations look in the dark.

3. Try putting a few fish near each other on a table, then turn out the lights and ask a friend to guess how many fish there are. Can your friend tell?

Sea the Point?

In the darkness of the deep sea, fish break up the outline of their bodies with patterns of light, making it hard for predators to figure out what they're really seeing. In Part 1, you should have found it was pretty tough for your friend to guess what a fish looked like when all that was visible were its lights!

In Part 2, you probably created some pretty confusing creatures. And you should have found that it was hard to tell where one fish ended and another began when all you could see were a bunch of glowing spots!

cut this shape out from one of your doughnut-shaped stickers

Life Under the Ice

Welcome to the chilly world of the polar seas, ocean explorer! It's hard to imagine that there's much going on below all the ice at the North and South Poles. But in fact, there are places where the water is downright crowded with life!

Plenty of Plankton

How can animals thrive in such a freezing cold place? In a word, plankton. These tiny creatures are an important source of food for marine animals, and they're 10 to 100 times more plentiful in polar oceans than in the rest of the watery world.

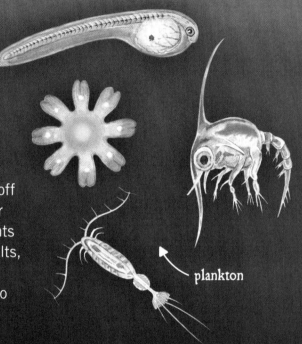

plankton

And what makes the polar oceans a good place for plankton to live? Well, plankton feed off of algae, and channels of water inside the polar ice are a great place for these microscopic plants to grow. In the spring when some of the ice melts, algae fills the water, turning it green, brown, or even red! Then algae-eating plankton move in to feast, followed by fish and whales (who eat the plankton), and so on up the food chain!

Underwater Icicles

If you could peek underneath a polar ice cap, you might see some things that look like icicles hanging below the ice. These are *ice stalactites*, frozen formations of hollow ice that can grow several feet long!

Unlike regular icicles, ice stalactites aren't solid ice—they're like tubes. They form when *very* salty water drains out of icebergs (this happens because the ice gets rid of the salt as it freezes). The temperature of the draining water is below freezing, but because the water is so salty, it stays liquid. When this super-cold salty water comes in contact with the less-salty ocean water below, it freezes that water, forming a tube around the draining salty water!

The Tip of Your Iceberg

It's hard to imagine the seas of the North and South Poles without icebergs. These giant, floating hunks of ice, which drift out to sea after breaking free from glaciers, vary from the size of a small piano to as big as the state of Connecticut! And if you think they look big from the ocean's surface, what till you see what icebergs are like *underwater*!

What You Need
- Iceberg mold
- Large bowl of water
- Large, clear pitcher or vase

What You Do

1. Open your iceberg mold and push it into a bowl of water, with both halves facing upward so they fill with water. Then, close the mold, sealing it completely on all sides.

2. Place your iceberg in the freezer with the larger half of the mold on the bottom. Prop your mold up with other items in the freezer so it doesn't tip over, and leave it in overnight.

3. When your iceberg has frozen, open up the mold and remove your 'berg. If you have trouble freeing the iceberg from the mold, run a little warm water over it.

4. To see how your iceberg floats, fill a pitcher with cold water and place your iceberg in. What happens?

Sea the Point?

You probably discovered that nearly all of your iceberg was under the water—only a very small portion of it floated above water. This is how real icebergs float, too! Just one-eighth of an iceberg pokes above water, while the rest of the massive ice chunk lies hidden below.

Icebergs can be beautiful—but also dangerous for humans. It's often hard for a ship passing through ice-filled waters to detect and avoid the huge, hidden parts of icebergs. But icebergs are a big help for many polar animals, who use them as resting places to warm themselves in the Sun and stay safe from predators.

Survive with Salt!

If any ordinary fish swam in polar waters, it would be in danger of freezing. But the fish who live near the poles are no ordinary fish! They have extra salt in their blood, which lowers their blood's freezing point. This means the blood stays liquid at colder temperatures instead of forming ice. In this Sea Quest, you'll see for yourself how salt keeps things liquid, then put your knowledge to work as you make your own ice cream!

What You Do

Part 1: Salt's Super-Power

Can salt really keep water from freezing? Try this and you'll see that it can!

1. Label three plastic cups 1, 2, and 3 with a marker. Then fill each cup with water, leaving a little bit of room at the top.

2. Put one tablespoon of salt in cup 1, two in cup 2, and none in cup 3. Stir the first two cups well so the salt dissolves.

3. Place all three cups in the freezer.

What You Need

- 3 plastic or paper cups
- Marker
- Water
- Salt
- Tablespoon
- 1-quart freezer bag with a zip closure
- ¼ cup sugar
- ½ cup milk
- ½ cup heavy cream
- ¼ teaspoon vanilla
- 2 cups crushed ice
- ¾ cup table salt or rock salt
- 1-gallon freezer bag with a zip closure
- Gloves or towel
- Bowls and spoons

4. Check on your cups every thirty minutes and inspect the water inside. Which cup's water stays liquid the longest?

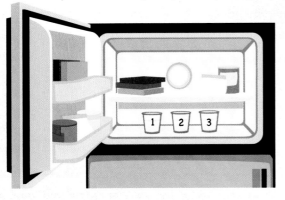

Part 2: Ice Cream Creation

Now that you've seen how salt can keep water from freezing, check out what else salt can do: Help make ice cream! Give it a try, then find out why salt makes ice cream cold.

I. Inside a quart-sized bag with a zip closure, combine the sugar, milk, heavy cream, and vanilla. Then seal the bag.

2. Put the ice and salt into a gallon-sized bag with a zip closure.

3. Place the sealed quart bag inside the gallon bag of ice and salt, then seal the gallon bag.

4. Rock the gallon bag from side to side to make sure your ice cream mixture freezes evenly. Wear gloves or wrap the bag in a towel to keep your hands warm!

5. Continue to rock the bag for ten to fifteen minutes, until the ice cream is solid.

6. Carefully remove the quart bag from the gallon bag, open it, spoon the ice cream into bowls, and chow down!

Sea the Point?

As you should have found in Part 1, salty water took longer to freeze than the salt-free water. And the more salt you added, the longer the water stayed liquid. This is because the salt lowered the freezing point of the water by getting in the way of the formation of ice crystals. This means the water had to get colder before it froze. That's why fish with salt in their blood can keep from freezing in the polar seas.

In Part 2, your ice cream ingredients needed to be colder than 32 degrees F (0 degrees C, the normal temperature of ice) in order to freeze into ice cream. And you made that happen by adding salt to the ice!

So how does salt make ice colder? First, the salt lowered the freezing point of the ice, causing it to melt. But ice needed heat in order to melt. In this case, it used heat from the other ice around it, meaning that all the ice got even colder than usual. The melting ice also used heat from the ice cream ingredients, making them super-cold—cold enough to freeze into ice cream!

Beat the Ice!

Polar ocean water is not just cold—it's *super* cold. The salt in seawater keeps ice crystals from forming, so salty ocean water can go as low as 28 degrees F (–2 degrees C) before icing up, unlike fresh water, which freezes at 32 degrees F (0 degrees C).

For animals that swim in polar oceans, these super-cold temperatures could be a real problem. Fortunately, fish and mammals that live in chilly regions have developed lots of ways to keep from freezing, like these:

Fill Up on Anti-Freeze Cold-water fish have a special chemical in their bodies that absorbs ice crystals. If ice starts to form inside their bodies, this chemical can get rid of the crystals before they can get big enough to cause problems. This works just like the anti-freeze that people put inside car engines!

Just Add Salt In addition to their own anti-freeze, fish also have salt in their blood that lowers the freezing temperature, as you discovered on pages 36–37. This helps to keep their blood fluid when it gets really cold.

Have a Heart Having a big heart, wide blood vessels, and thin blood also helps to keep blood flowing fast when it's frigid.

Be a Blubber Belly Marine mammals like whales, walruses, and seals have a thick layer of fat, called blubber, to keep them warm.

Be Big! The bigger you are, the less exposed skin you have per pound, which helps keep your body heat from escaping. This technique works great for warm-blooded creatures like whales, penguins, and polar bears. Try the Sea Quest on page 40 to prove that bigger is better when it's bitter cold!

Polar Survival
Strategies

In addition to the ways their bodies help keep them warm, there are lots of things that polar animals can do to make freezing temperatures easier to bear. It's all about getting as much food and burning as little energy as possible— kind of like being a couch potato! Here's how some animals handle the cold:

- **Have Small Families**
  Taking care of kids can be tiring, especially since the babies of polar mammals, like whales and polar bears, stay with their mothers for a long time. So, polar parents like the beluga whale only have one baby at a time.

a beluga mom and her baby

leopard seal

- **Don't Be a Picky Eater**
  Some cold-water creatures will climb lower down the food chain to keep their bellies bulging. Increasing your menu options decreases your chances of going hungry. Even the fearsome leopard seal, which often hunts down penguins and other seals, will feed on tiny krill when other food is scarce.

- **Hibernate**
  Just like animals in the forest, lots of polar animals hibernate, which means they store up energy by staying in an inactive, sleep-like state in caves and dens throughout the winter. Polar hibernators range from giant polar bears to tiny Arctic ground squirrels.

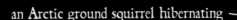
an Arctic ground squirrel hibernating

Stay Warm by Being Big

Big animals have a big advantage where it's cold. Warm-blooded animals like whales and polar bears can stay warm more easily the bigger they are. Want to see for yourself how being bigger means staying warmer? Try out this Sea Quest!

What You Need

- 1 large plastic cup
- 1 small plastic cup
- Water

What You Do

1. Fill a large cup and a small cup each three-quarters full with warm water.

2. Place both cups in the freezer.

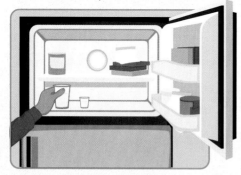

3. Every ten minutes, return to the freezer and dip a finger into each cup. Which one feels colder? Which one freezes first?

Sea the Point?

The water in the small cup froze a lot faster than the water in the large cup, right? This happens because large containers can hold a lot more stuff inside them. And the more stuff inside an object, the better it can hang onto heat.

Think of it this way: If you were standing in a cold place all alone, you'd get chilly pretty fast. But if you were huddled together with ten friends, creating a bigger mass, you'd all stay warmer. Well, bigger animals (and bigger cups of water) stay warmer for the same reason!

The polar bear, which can weigh up to 1,764 pounds (800 kg), is the biggest bear in the world.

Arctic vs. Antarctic

The Arctic and the Antarctic. Their names sound alike, and they're both cold places, so they're pretty much the same, right? Wrong! In fact, they're far more different than they are alike.

Here's what's the same: They're both really cold and dry, and both have lots of icebergs, whales, seals, birds, fish, and krill. They're also roughly the same size (about twenty times the size of Texas).

Here's what's different:

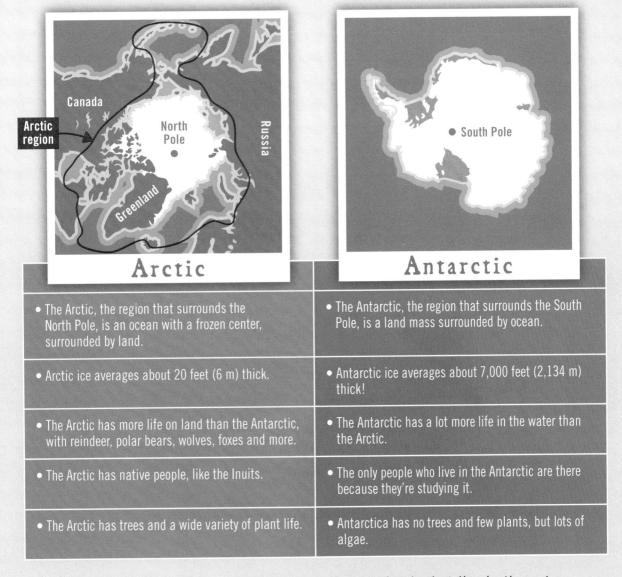

Arctic	Antarctic
• The Arctic, the region that surrounds the North Pole, is an ocean with a frozen center, surrounded by land.	• The Antarctic, the region that surrounds the South Pole, is a land mass surrounded by ocean.
• Arctic ice averages about 20 feet (6 m) thick.	• Antarctic ice averages about 7,000 feet (2,134 m) thick!
• The Arctic has more life on land than the Antarctic, with reindeer, polar bears, wolves, foxes and more.	• The Antarctic has a lot more life in the water than the Arctic.
• The Arctic has native people, like the Inuits.	• The only people who live in the Antarctic are there because they're studying it.
• The Arctic has trees and a wide variety of plant life.	• Antarctica has no trees and few plants, but lots of algae.

On the next few pages, you'll get to know the animals that live in these two regions, starting with a trip up north to the Arctic!

Arctic Animals:

polar bear

Welcome to the Arctic! Life in this region runs from tiny plankton to huge bowhead whales. In between are some amazing animals, such as:

- **Polar bears.** These fierce predators can run up to 25 miles per hour (40 km/h). Underneath their blanket of white fur (which helps them blend in with the snow and ice), they have black skin (which helps absorb heat) and up to 4 inches (10 cm) of fat to protect them from the cold.

- **Arctic terns.** These birds make the longest migration of any bird in the world. These frequent fliers soar from the Arctic to the Antarctic and back every year—that's a 21,750-mile (35,000-km) round trip. Yet they weigh less than a pound!

- **Greenland sharks.** These sharks are known as "sleeper sharks" because they swim so slowly in the icy Arctic waters. How they manage to eat so many fish, squid, and seals is a bit of a mystery. But it may be because glow-in-the-dark creatures called copepods (COPE-eh-pods) attach themselves to the sharks' eyes, which may attract prey.

Greenland shark

Chillin' at the North Pole

Arctic tern

Arctic char

- **Arctic char.** When they're young, these fish eat plankton. When they get bigger, they eat small Arctic char! Actually, it isn't that unusual for fish to eat members of their own species, and it happens mostly when there's nothing else for them to eat.

- **Humpback whales.** These whales grow up to 52 feet (16 m) long and are known for being the most beautiful and noisiest singers in the sea. They migrate to the Arctic in the summer to feed, then head to warmer waters for the winter, where they live off their layer of blubber. These whales often hunt together, forcing huge masses of prey to the surface by blowing huge walls of bubbles. Then they chow down!

humpback whale

spiny lumpsucker

- **Spiny lumpsuckers.** These bottom-dwelling fish are covered with cone-shaped bumps. They use a powerful suction cup on their bottom fins to stick to rocks, eating anything that swims within eating range.

emperor penguins

Antarctic Animals:

Welcome to Antarctica, ocean explorer! This region is colder, icier, and a lot lonelier (at least for people) than the Arctic. The surprise is that the Antarctic food chain is packed with predators and prey—everything from tiny krill to fish, birds, seals, and whales. Here are just a few of the animals you'll find near the South Pole:

- **Emperor penguins.** These are the world's biggest penguins—they can be as tall as 3.8 feet (1.2 meters) and as heavy as 88 pounds (40 kg). Being so big helps them stay warm, as you learned on page 40! These penguins can dive 1,500 feet (500 meters) down and hold their breath for up to twenty-two minutes, which allows them to reach food other birds can't.

- **Ice fish.** These fish have clear blood! Why? It's because they have no hemoglobin, the substance that makes blood red and carries oxygen through the bloodstream. Hemoglobin doesn't work so well in freezing cold water, so ice fish have developed ways to do without it. They're the only vertebrates on the planet that completely lack hemoglobin!

ice fish

- **Antarctic krill.** These little guys spend their days in the deep ocean, but swim up to the surface at night to feed on plankton. They can go up to 200 days without eating. Meanwhile, they get eaten in huge numbers by many Antarctic species.

krill

A Chock-Full Food Chain

wandering albatross

crab-eater seal

- **Crab-eater seals.** There are more of these than any other large mammal on Earth—except people. They were misnamed by the French explorers who discovered them, because they don't eat crabs (there are no crabs in Antarctica!). They *do*, however, eat about 45 pounds (20 kg) of krill every day. These seals take in mouthfuls of seawater, then spit out the water (but not the krill) between their upper and lower teeth, which form a natural strainer.

- **Wandering albatross.** These birds will go as far as it takes for a good meal, sometimes flying round trips of thousands of miles to bring food back to their young. They can live as long as eighty-five years, and they probably fly farther in a lifetime than any other bird. Sailors believed it was bad luck to kill one because they thought they carried the souls of dead sailors.

- **Killer whales.** Also known as orcas, these are the largest meat-eaters on Earth, and 70 percent of all killer whales live in Antarctica. They are incredible hunters, feeding on everything from fish to young seals to other whales.

killer whale

So, ocean explorer, have you ever wondered why penguins are dressed in "tuxedos"? Turn the page to find out why being black and white helps them survive in the Antarctic!

Heat and Light in Black and White

If a penguin wants to hide from a predator amid all the snow and ice of Antarctica, its black back isn't going to help it blend in! So what *is* that black back good for? For one thing, it helps the penguin stay warm. Try this Sea Quest to see why.

What You Do

1. Place a piece of black paper and a piece of white paper next to each other under a desk lamp.

2. Turn on the lamp, making sure that its bulb is just a few inches away from the papers. Center the lamp between the two papers so they get an equal amount of light, and leave the lamp on for about ten minutes.

3. Come back and place one hand on each piece of paper. What do you notice?

What You Need

- Piece of white paper
- Piece of black paper
- Desk lamp

Sea the Point?

The black paper was much warmer than the white paper, right? That's because the color black absorbs heat and light, while white reflects it. Penguins use this to their advantage! When they're cold, they turn their black backs toward the Sun to absorb as much heat as possible. If they feel too warm, they turn their white bellies to the Sun, reflecting most of the light away!

These penguins are warming themselves in the Sun after a swim.

MARINE BIOLOGIST
Dr. Bodil Bluhm

Meet **Dr. Bodil Bluhm** (BAHD-il BLOOM), a marine biologist who studies the animals and food chains in the Arctic Ocean. She got hooked on life around and under the ice after taking a ferry trip through the ice of the Baltic Sea when she was in high school. She now teaches at the University of Alaska at Fairbanks and studies the Arctic seafloor with remote-control underwater vehicles known as *remotely operated vehicles* (ROVs).

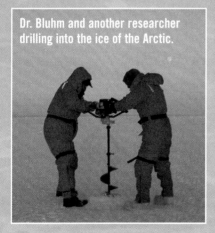

Dr. Bluhm and another researcher drilling into the ice of the Arctic.

Question: What's so exciting about exploring the Arctic?

Answer: Not only is the Arctic a beautiful, magical, and icy place, it also affects ocean currents and climate around the world. It's a challenging area to work in because it's so cold and hard to get to, and there's a lot we still don't know about it.

Q: What's it like to be the first person ever to see a particular part of the ocean floor?

A: In 2002, I was part of a group that was the first to explore the seafloor of the Arctic Canada Basin, north of Alaska. We were clinging to the screen as we watched a live video from our vehicle's camera. We recognized fish, brittle stars, and anemones, and we saw creatures that had never been seen before!

One of the fish that Dr. Bluhm saw on the seafloor of the Arctic Canada Basin.

Q: What's the greatest threat facing animals that live under the ice?

A: The biggest problem right now is climate change. There's less and less ice floating in the sea, which endangers the lives of animals and plants that live in or on the ice. And once the ice has melted enough to allow cargo ships to pass through, there will be new hazards, like more pollutants.

Q: What's the strangest thing you've ever discovered while exploring the seafloor?

A: We once found a few hundred fish ear bones, without the rest of the fish—and after analyzing them, we determined that they were several thousand years old! Was there a mass death of fish once upon a time? Were the ocean currents funneling all ear bones of dead fish to this one spot for some reason? What happened? We just don't know.

Extreme Ocean Expert

Congratulations, ocean explorer, your journey to the extremes of the ocean is complete—consider yourself an expert! You've seen the sea at its deepest depths and discovered the wild world waiting there—with astounding animals, huge seamounts, bubbling volcanic vents, and more!

You *also* traveled under the ice, where you met animals that can stay warm even in below-freezing conditions. And now you know that while the Arctic and the Antarctic are both really cold, there are big differences between them!

There are still plenty of mysteries about the ocean's extremes to be uncovered—and maybe someday you'll be the one discovering new species on the ocean floor or under the ice!

THE ANSWER KEY

▶ Pages 8–9: **See the Seafloor**
   1) B   **2)** A   **3)** B   **4)** C

▶ Pages 20–21: **Figure Out the Food Web**

Octopus

Vent Crab

Tube Worm

Vent Clam

Vent Shrimp

Vent Bacteria